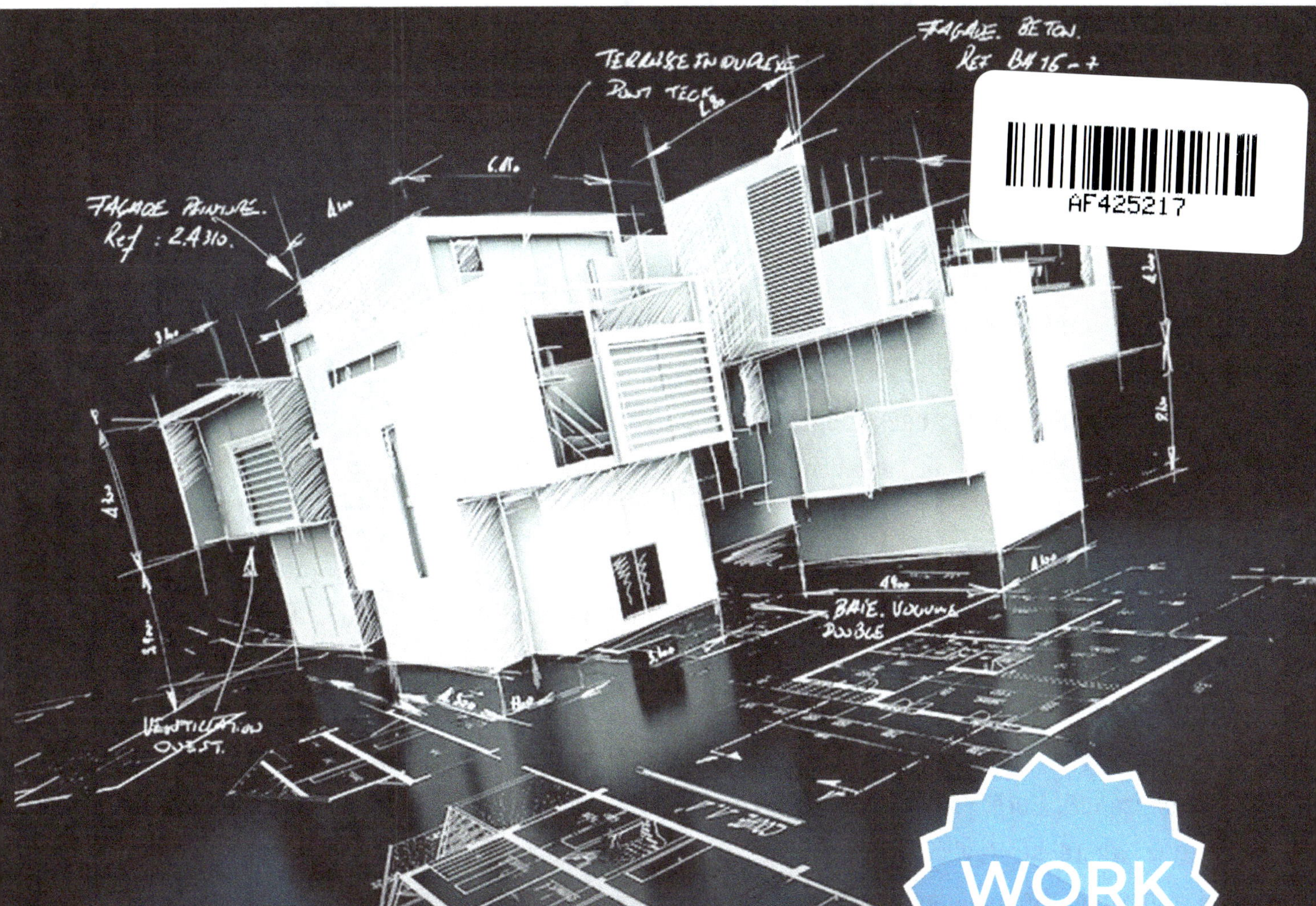

THE REAL ESTATE *Agent*

BLUEPRINT

A WORKBOOK FOR ASPIRING AND THRIVING REAL ESTATE AGENTS

GINA NASH

In the world of real estate, where ambition knows no bounds and dreams become reality, this workbook serves as your trusted guide. It has been meticulously crafted through the crucible of ambition and refined by the crucible of experience.

As you step into the dynamic realm of the real estate industry, envision this workbook as your unwavering companion—a compass that will navigate you through the uncharted waters from hopeful aspiration to triumphant realization. Here, you will embark on an exhilarating journey, one where strategic planning meets calculated execution, and where the roadmap to your real estate odyssey unfolds in vibrant detail.

This workbook is more than just a tool; it's a treasure trove of insights from industry titans and market pioneers. It equips you with practical tools to ascend to new heights in your real estate career. Whether you're a newcomer eagerly standing on the threshold of possibility or a seasoned pro looking to elevate your game, this workbook is your catalyst for tangible success. Your aspirations lay the foundation, and your dreams form the blueprint for your journey.

Together, we will embark on this transformative adventure. Picture your ambitions as a canvas waiting to be painted, and let the brushstrokes of reality create a masterpiece of achievement and fulfillment. Welcome to your real estate odyssey. Welcome to your personal blueprint for success.

GINA NASH

TABLE OF CONTENT

CHAPTER 1
INTRODUCTION TO THE REAL ESTATE INDUSTRY

Your Role as a Real Estate Agent

Definition and Purpose

As a real estate agent, your primary role is to act as a professional intermediary between buyers and sellers in real estate transactions. Your expertise, knowledge, and guidance play a vital role in helping clients navigate the complex process of buying, selling, or renting properties. Your ultimate goal is to facilitate successful transactions while ensuring the best possible outcomes for your clients.

Core Responsibilities:

Property Listing and Marketing:

- Prepare accurate property listings that highlight key features and benefits.
- Develop and execute effective marketing strategies to attract potential buyers or renters.
- Use various platforms, including online listings, social media, and traditional marketing channels, to maximize property exposure.

GINA NASH

Client Representation:

- Represent sellers by showcasing their properties to interested buyers.
- Assist buyers in finding properties that match their preferences, needs, and budget.
- Act as a liaison between clients and other agents, facilitating negotiations and communication.

Market Knowledge and Analysis:

- Stay up-to-date with the latest trends, property values, and market conditions.
- Provide clients with accurate pricing insights and neighborhood information.
- Analyze market data to offer informed advice on property value and investment potential.

Negotiation and Deal Structuring:

- Skillfully negotiate offers and counteroffers on behalf of clients.
- Use your negotiation expertise to secure favorable terms and pricing for your clients.
- Structure deals that align with your clients' goals and financial capabilities.

Documentation and Legal Compliance:

- Prepare and review contracts, agreements, and other legal documents.
- Ensure that all paperwork is completed accurately and adheres to legal requirements.
- Guide clients through the documentation process, addressing any questions or concerns.

Property Showings and Presentations:

- Schedule and conduct property viewings for potential buyers or renters.
- Highlight the unique features and benefits of each property to attract interest.
- Provide professional presentations that showcase properties in the best light.

Client Consultation and Communication:

- Engage in active listening to understand clients' needs, preferences, and objectives.
- Provide personalized advice and guidance to help clients make informed decisions.
- Maintain open and transparent communication throughout the entire transaction process.

GINA NASH

Networking and Collaborations:
- Build and nurture a network of industry professionals, including lenders, appraisers, inspectors, and other agents.
- Collaborate with fellow agents to expand your reach and increase opportunities for successful transactions.

Problem Solving and Creative Solutions:
- Anticipate and address challenges that may arise during transactions, such as financing issues or property inspections.
- Offer creative solutions to overcome obstacles and keep transactions on track.

Ethical Standards and Client Focused Approach:
- Uphold a high level of professionalism and adhere to a strict code of ethics.
- Always prioritize the best interests of your clients, maintaining confidentiality and integrity.

NOTES

____

____

____

____

____

Personal Qualities and Skills:

To excel in your role as a real estate agent, you should possess or develop the following qualities and skills:

- **Communication Skills:** Effective verbal and written communication to convey information clearly to clients, other agents, and professionals.
- **Negotiation Expertise:** Strong negotiation skills to secure favorable terms for your clients while maintaining a positive rapport.
- **Market Expertise:** In-depth knowledge of the local real estate market, including trends, property values, and neighborhood dynamics.
- **Problem-Solving Abilities:** The ability to identify challenges and develop innovative solutions to ensure smooth transactions.
- **Attention to Detail:** A keen eye for details to ensure accurate documentation and a thorough understanding of contract terms.
- **Time Management:** Efficiently manage your time to handle multiple tasks, property showings, and client interactions.
- **Client-Centric Approach:** A genuine desire to help clients achieve their real estate goals, building trust and long-term relationships.
- **Tech Savviness:** Familiarity with technology and online tools used in the real estate industry for listings, marketing, and communication.

NOTES

____

____

____

____

GINA NASH

Benefits and Rewards:

Your role as a real estate agent offers several benefits and rewards:

- **Earning Potential:** Real estate agents often have the opportunity to earn a commission-based income, which can be lucrative based on successful transactions.
- **Flexibility:** The flexibility to set your own schedule and manage your workload according to your preferences.
- **Personal Fulfillment:** The satisfaction of helping clients navigate important life decisions and achieve their real estate dreams.
- **Continuous Learning:** The real estate industry is dynamic, offering ongoing opportunities for learning and professional growth.
- **Networking Opportunities:** Building a network of industry contacts can lead to collaborative partnerships and increased business opportunities.

Exploring different real estate niches

Research and identify two distinct real estate niches that interest you.

☐ ____

☐ ____

Exercise: Write a paragraph about how you plan to specialize in one niche while still understanding the other.

____

____

____

____

____

____

Here's a list of different real estate niches to consider

1.Residential Real Estate:
- Representing buyers and sellers in residential property transactions.
- Includes single-family homes, condos, townhouses, and multifamily .

2. Commercial Real Estate:
- Dealing with office spaces, retail properties, and industrial properties
- Assisting clients in buying, selling, leasing, or investing in commercial properties

3. Luxury Real Estate:

- Catering to high-net-worth individuals interested in luxury homes and estates.
- Requires an understanding of luxury market trends and exceptional customer service.

4. Investment Properties:

- Assisting clients in identifying and acquiring income-generating properties.
- Involves analyzing potential returns and providing insights on investment opportunities.

5. Vacation and Second Homes:

- Focusing on clients looking to buy or sell vacation properties or second homes.
- Requires knowledge of local tourism trends and rental potential.

6. Senior Real Estate:

- Specializing in properties for seniors, such as retirement communities and assisted living homes.
- Navigating unique needs and considerations of senior clients.

7. First-Time Homebuyers:

- Guiding individuals or families through the process of buying their first home.
- Providing educational resources and support for newcomers to the real estate market.

8. Military Relocation:

- Assisting military personnel and their families with relocating due to deployments or assignments.
- Requires familiarity with military relocation programs and timelines.

9. New Construction:

- Collaborating with builders and developers to market and sell new construction properties.
- Understanding construction timelines, materials, and the customization process. .

10. Condo and Co-op Specialists:

- Focusing on buyers and sellers interested in condominiums and co-operative apartments.
- Understanding condo association rules, fees, and amenities.

11. International Real Estate:

- Working with clients interested in purchasing properties in foreign countries.
- Navigating international regulations, currency exchange, and legal considerations.

12. Distressed Properties:

- Dealing with foreclosures, short sales, and properties in distress.
- Requires knowledge of distressed property transactions and negotiation skills.

> **Choosing the right niche depends on your interests, strengths, and the local real estate market. Specializing in a niche can help you stand out, build expertise, and attract clients who are specifically looking for your services.**

NOTES

Market Trends and Dynamics

In recent years, there has been a growing trend of increased demand for sustainable and environmentally friendly homes. Buyers are showing interest in properties that incorporate energy-efficient features such as solar panels, smart thermostats, and eco-friendly construction materials. This trend is driven by both environmental awareness and the potential for long-term cost savings on utilities.

What are market trends and dynamics in real estate?

Answer: Market trends and dynamics refer to the patterns, shifts, and factors that influence the behavior of the real estate market. They impact property values, demand, supply, and overall market conditions.

How can real estate agents leverage market trends?

Answer: Real estate agents can use market trend insights to:

- Price properties accurately for sellers.
- Advise buyers on suitable purchase opportunities.
- Create effective marketing strategies based on current demand.
- Forecast potential shifts that could impact clients' investments.

List some resources of how you can find market trends in your area

Identifying Market Trends in Your Local Real Estate Market

Objective: To analyze and identify current market trends in the local real estate market and gain insights into the preferences of buyers and sellers. Instructions:

Select an Area: Choose a specific neighborhood or area within your city or region as the focus of your analysis.

Data Collection: Gather relevant data from local real estate listings, market reports, and government sources. Consider data such as:

- Property listings and their features (e.g., number of bedrooms, square footage, amenities).
- Recent property sales prices and time on market.
- Any new construction or developments in the area.

____

____

____

____

Identify Trends: Analyze the collected data to identify trends that are currently affecting the local real estate market. Look for patterns related to:

- **Pricing trends:** Are property prices rising, stabilizing, or declining?
- **Property features:** Are there specific features that are consistently in demand (e.g., open floor plans, outdoor spaces)?
- **Days on market:** How quickly are properties selling in the area?
- **Property types:** Are certain property types (e.g., condos, single-family homes) more popular than others?

____

____

____

____

NOTES

GINA NASH

CHAPTER 2
GETTING STARTED

Finding the right real estate brokerage and mentor can greatly contribute to your success as a real estate agent. Here are some techniques to assist you in this process:

1. Research:

- Conduct thorough online research to identify reputable brokerages in your area.
- Read reviews and testimonials from agents who have worked with these brokerages.
- Look into their market presence, support services, training programs, and company culture.

2. Interview Brokerages or Real Estate Teams:

- Set up meetings or interviews with representatives from potential brokerages.
- Ask about their training and mentorship programs, commission structure, and available resources.
- Inquire about their agents' success stories and support for new agents.

3. Research Mentorship Programs:

- Inquire about mentorship programs offered by different brokerages.
- Understand the structure, frequency of interactions, and expectations from mentors.
- Ask for success stories from agents who have benefited from their

4. Seek Transparency:

- Ensure that the brokerage and mentor are transparent about their expectations and commitment.
- Discuss how often you'll meet with your mentor and what kind of guidance they can provide.

5. Personal Compatibility:

- Choose a brokerage and mentor whose values, work style, and goals align with yours.
- A good mentor-mentee relationship is based on mutual respect and understanding.

6. Evaluate Opportunities:

- Consider the growth opportunities offered by the brokerage and mentor.
- Look for a balance between support for new agents and opportunities for advancement as you gain experience.

List your Top 5 Brokerages or Real Estate Teams you would like to interview

I.____

Why____

____

2.____

Why____

____

GINA NASH

3.____

Why____

____

4.____

Why____

____

5.____

Why____

____

Crafting a unique value proposition (UVP) as a real estate agent is crucial to stand out in a competitive market. Your UVP communicates what sets you apart from other agents and why clients should choose you. Here's a step-by-step guide to help you create an effective UVP:

Step 1: Identify Your Strengths and Expertise

- **Self-Assessment:** Reflect on your skills, experience, and unique qualities. What do you excel at as a real estate agent? What sets you apart from others?

____

____

____

____

____

- **Niche Expertise:** Determine if you have expertise in a specific niche (e.g., luxury homes, first-time buyers, investment properties) that can differentiate you.

____

____

____

____

____

Step 2: Understand Your Target Audience

- **Buyer Persona:** Define your ideal clients. What are their needs, pain points, and preferences? Tailor your UVP to address their specific concerns.

____

____

____

____

Step 3: Define Your UVP Components

- **Problem-Solution:** Identify the challenges your clients face and how you solve them. What unique solutions do you offer?

____

____

____

____

- **Benefits:** List the tangible and intangible benefits clients gain from working with you. This could include time savings, personalized guidance, or peace of mind.

____

____

____

____

- **Differentiators:** Highlight what makes you stand out. It could be your experience, market knowledge, technology integration, or innovative marketing strategies.

____

____

____

____

Step 4: Craft Your UVP Statement

- **Clear and Concise:** Your UVP should be brief and easy to understand. Aim for a single sentence or a short paragraph.

____

____

____

____

____

- **Value-Centric Language:** Use language that emphasizes the value you provide to clients.
- **Emotional Appeal:** Incorporate emotional elements that resonate with clients, such as trust, security, or achieving their dreams.

 GINA NASH

NOTES

CHAPTER 3
BUILDING A STRONG FOUNDATION

Task: Develop a one-year business plan including income goals and marketing strategies.

____

____

____

____

____

Example: Generate $100,000 in commission. Pros: Clear roadmap, Cons: Might need adjustments

Exercise: Detail how you'll diversify income sources

____

____

____

____

7 Essential Components of a Real Estate Business Plan

Mission statement: Clearly define your purpose and the benefit you provide.

SWOT analysis: SWOT (Strengths, Weaknesses, Opportunities, and Threats) is an assessment of you as an agent and of the landscape where you practice.

Specific goals: Separate your goals into short-term and long-term to ensure that your short-term goals support the long-term.

Strategic plan: Determine what specific strategies you will use to achieve your goals. Your business plan should evolve as your business and abilities grow.

Time frame: Determine a time frame to achieve each of your goals and to help you stay accountable and focused.

Target audience: Define your audience and your market to help you refine your strategies.

Systems and processes: Have specific systems to achieve your goals. For example, use a customer relationship management system to keep track of clients and their needs.

©2017 National Association of REALTORS®
Source: Real Estate Express, "Grow Your Real Estate Career: 7 Components of a Real Estate Business Plan", 2017

GINA NASH

Executive Summary:

_________________________________ is an experienced and dedicated real estate agent committed to providing exceptional service to clients in_____________________. With _______ years of experience and a deep understanding of the local market, our goal is to deliver personalized solutions that meet the unique needs of buyers and sellers. Our services include property listings, buyer representation, negotiation expertise, and market insights.

Mission Statement:

____

____

____

____

____

Vision:

____

____

____

____

____

Services:

____

____

____

____

Target Market:

____

____

____

____

Marketing Strategy:

____

____

____

____

Competitive Advantage:

____

____

____

____

Financial Projections:

Year 1:

- Projected Sales: $____________________
- Operating Expenses: $________________
- Net Income: $______________________

Year 2:

- Projected Sales: $____________________
- Operating Expenses: $________________
- Net Income: $______________________

Year 3:

- Projected Sales:$ ____________________
- Operating Expenses: $________________
- Net Income: $______________________

Growth Strategy:

- Expand the client base by nurturing referrals and positive word-of-mouth.
- Attend local networking events to connect with potential clients and industry professionals.
- Consider partnerships with mortgage brokers and home inspectors to offer comprehensive services.

Step 1: Assess Current Financial Situation

- Calculate your current income, expenses, and savings.

  - Income: $_______________________

  - Expenses: $_______________________

  - Savings: $_______________________

- List your existing business expenses (marketing, office supplies, transportation).

  - Business Expenses: $_______________________

- Analyze your existing client base and sales data.

  - _______________________

Step 2: Set Growth Goals

- Define specific growth goals (e.g., increase monthly sales by X%, expand client base by Y%).

  ____

  ____

- Estimate the additional income required to meet these goals._______________________

  ____

GINA NASH

Step 3: Create a Realistic Budget

- Detail your projected income sources (commissions, referral fees).______________________

  ____

- List expected business expenses for marketing, professional development, and operations.

  ____

  ____.

Step 4: Plan for Marketing Expenses

- Allocate a portion of your budget for marketing activities (social media, advertising, branding).

  ____

  ____

- Set clear goals for marketing campaigns (increased website traffic, lead generation).

  ____

  ____

Step 5: Monitor and Adjust

- Regularly track your actual income and expenses against your budget. ______________

  ____

- Compare your financial performance with your growth goals and make adjustments as needed.

____

____

Step 6: Prepare for Savings and Taxes

- Allocate a percentage of your income for savings (emergency fund, retirement).

____

____

- Estimate quarterly tax payments and set funds aside accordingly.

____

____

____

NOTES

CHAPTER 4
EFFECTIVE MARKETING STRATEGIES

Task: Design a personal brand logo and create social media profiles.

Makc a notc of what you would likc your logo to look likc:

____

____

____

____

____

GINA NASH

Write a caption for your first social media post.

____

____

____

____

Determine how often you would begin posting on your social platforms:

____

____

____

____

GINA NASH

In the dynamic world of real estate, leveraging social media for lead generation is a powerful strategy to connect with potential clients and grow your business. Here's how to effectively utilize social media platforms to attract and convert leads:

1. Choose the Right Platforms:

- Identify Your Ideal Clients: Determine which social media platforms your target audience, such as homebuyers, sellers, and investors, frequent the most. Platforms like Facebook, Instagram, LinkedIn, and Twitter are particularly useful for real estate agents.

2. Optimize Your Profiles:

- Professional Presence: Ensure your profiles present a professional image. Use a high-quality profile picture and craft a compelling bio that showcases your real estate expertise.

3. Create Valuable Content:

- Educate and Inform: Share informative content about the local real estate market, insights on neighborhoods, tips for buyers and sellers, and updates on market trends.
- Visual Impact: Utilize captivating images, videos, virtual property tours, and eye-catching infographics to showcase properties and demonstrate your industry knowledge.

4. Engage Your Audience:

- Timely Responses: Promptly respond to comments, messages, and inquiries to demonstrate your commitment and build rapport with potential leads.
- Engagement Tactics: Initiate discussions, ask questions, and encourage interaction on your posts to keep your audience engaged.

GINA NASH

5. Utilize Lead Generation Tools:

- Effective CTAs: Incorporate clear and compelling Calls-to-Action (CTAs) in your posts, guiding users to take action such as contacting you for more details or scheduling a consultation.
- Dedicated Landing Pages: Develop dedicated landing pages on your website to showcase specific properties or campaigns and include links in your social media posts.
- Lead Forms: Take advantage of lead generation forms provided by platforms like Facebook and Instagram to gather potential leads' information directly within the platform.

6. Run Targeted Ads:

- Targeted Outreach: Define your target audience precisely, considering factors such as demographics, interests, location, and behaviors.
- Visual Impact: Utilize various ad formats, such as photo ads, carousel ads, videos, or story ads, to effectively display your listings and services.
- Retargeting Strategies: Reconnect with users who have previously engaged with your content or visited your website through retargeting ads.

7. Provide Value with Free Resources:

- Educational Content: Create downloadable resources like ebooks on the home buying/selling process, market trends, or local guides in exchange for contact information.
- Interactive Sessions: Host live webinars or Q&A sessions where you share your real estate insights, answer queries, and interact directly with potential leads.

8. Analytics and Optimization:

- Data-Driven Decisions: Regularly analyze the performance metrics provided by social media platforms to gauge the effectiveness of your content and campaigns.
- Refine Strategies: Use the insights gained from analytics to refine your content strategy and optimize your lead generation efforts.

9. Build Lasting Relationships:

- Nurturing Leads: Engage with your generated leads through personalized messages or informative email newsletters, offering value and building a sense of trust.
- Personal Touch: Showcase your authenticity and demonstrate your genuine interest in assisting your followers with their real estate needs.

By skillfully harnessing social media, real estate agents can establish a strong online presence, attract potential clients, and cultivate meaningful relationships that lead to successful transactions and long-term business growth.

NOTES

CHAPTER 5
LEAD GENERATION AND PROSPECTING

Identify three lead sources and outline strategies for each.

1. ____

____

____

2. ____

____

____

3. ____

____

____

Exploring different lead sources

Here's a simple and easy-to-understand guide on exploring different lead sources as a real estate agent, along with the best ways to utilize each source:

Exploring Different Lead Sources for Real Estate Agents

As a real estate agent, tapping into various lead sources can significantly boost your business. Here are some key lead sources and the best ways to leverage them:

1. For Sale By Owner (FSBO)

Source: Homeowners selling their property without an agent's representation.

Best Way to Use: Approach FSBOs with professionalism and value. Offer your expertise, market knowledge, and negotiation skills. Emphasize the convenience and efficiency of working with a professional agent.

2. Expired Listings

Source: Listings that were listed but didn't sell during the agreed-upon timeframe.

Best Way to Use: Reach out to homeowners whose listings have expired. Showcase your marketing strategies, fresh perspective, and determination to help them achieve their goal of selling their property.

3. Referrals

Source: Recommendations from past clients, friends, family, and industry professionals.

Best Way to Use: Nurture relationships with satisfied clients, and ask for referrals. Provide excellent service to encourage word-of-mouth recommendations. Stay in touch with a regular newsletter or updates.

4. Online Leads

Source: Leads generated through your website, social media, and online advertising.

Best Way to Use: Optimize your website for lead capture with clear CTAs. Engage with leads on social media platforms by sharing valuable content. Respond promptly to inquiries and use automated follow-up systems.

5. Open Houses

Source: Prospective buyers and sellers who attend open house events.

Best Way to Use: Host engaging open houses with well-presented properties. Collect visitors' information and follow up with them after the event. Provide insights about the property, neighborhood, and market trends

6. Networking Events

Source: Contacts made at local real estate or community events.

Best Way to Use: Attend networking events to connect with potential clients, other agents, and industry professionals. Engage in genuine conversations and share your expertise without being overly sales-oriented

7. Expired Rental Listings

Source: Rental listings that have been listed but not rented.

Best Way to Use: Reach out to property owners who have struggled to rent their properties. Offer insights into the market and present the potential benefits of selling the property instead.

8. Social Media Engagement

Source: Engaging with followers and connections on social media platforms.

Best Way to Use: Respond to comments and messages promptly. Participate in discussions, answer questions, and provide value to your audience. Build trust and establish yourself as a knowledgeable resource

NOTES

____

____

____

____

____

____

Lead Source Utilization Form:

Lead Source	Best Approach
FSBO	Provide expertise, negotiation skills, and advantages of professional representation.
Expired Listings	Offer fresh perspective, marketing strategies, and commitment to selling their property.
Referrals	Nurture relationships, ask for referrals, and maintain excellent service for word-of-mouth.
Online Leads	Optimize website for lead capture, engage on social media, and respond promptly to inquiries
Open Houses	Host engaging events, collect visitor information, and provide insights about properties.
Networking Events	Attend events, engage genuinely, and share industry knowledge without excessive selling.
Expired Rental Listings	Offer insights into the market and present the benefits of selling instead of renting.
Social Media Engagement	Respond to comments, answer questions, and provide value through your expertise.

GINA NASH

What Lead Sources would you most likely to work with?

____

____

____

____

NOTES

____

____

____

____

____

GINA NASH

CHAPTER 6
MASTERING CLIENT RELATIONSHIPS

List three active listening techniques and practice with a friend.*

1. ____

____

2. ____

____

3. ____

____

Here are some good ways to effectively manage client expectations:

1. Clear Communication:

- Maintain open and honest communication from the start.
- Explain the process, timelines, and potential challenges upfront.
- Set regular communication channels (email, phone, in-person) and stick to them.

2. Educate About the Process:

- Provide a step-by-step overview of the buying/selling process.
- Educate clients about market trends, local regulations, and common issues.

3. Understand Their Needs:

- Listen actively to your clients' goals, preferences, and concerns.
- Tailor your approach to match their specific requirements.

4. Realistic Pricing:

- Provide a realistic market analysis to set the right price expectations.
- Be transparent about how pricing affects their chances of a successful transaction.

5. Property Selection:

- Help buyers understand that no property is perfect and compromises may be necessary.
- Guide sellers on how to prepare their property for the market to attract the right buyers.

GINA NASH

6. Market Conditions:

- Explain how market conditions can impact their buying/selling experience.
- Keep them updated about changes in the market that may affect their transaction.

7. Negotiation Realities:

- Explain that negotiations are a part of the process.
- Prepare them for potential counteroffers and provide negotiation strategies.

8. Timelines and Delays:

- Set realistic expectations about the time it takes to find a property or close a deal.
- Inform clients that delays can occur due to inspections, appraisals, or other factors

9. Legal and Contractual Aspects:

- Simplify legal jargon and explain contract terms clearly.
- Stress the importance of adhering to deadlines and fulfilling contractual obligations.

10. Emotional Rollercoaster:

- Acknowledge that buying or selling a home can be emotionally challenging.
- Offer reassurance and support during stressful moments.

11. Technology Usage:

- Educate clients on how you'll use technology for efficient communication and document sharing.
- Offer tutorials if needed to ensure they're comfortable with the tools.

12. Provide Options:

- Present alternative solutions when faced with challenges.
- Discuss potential scenarios and their consequences.

13. Stay Accessible:

- Be available to address their questions and concerns promptly.
- Use modern communication tools to facilitate easy contact.

14. Feedback Loop:

- Regularly check in with clients to ensure their expectations are being met.
- Address any misunderstandings or concerns promptly.

15. Post-Transaction Support:

- Offer guidance even after the transaction is complete.
- Help clients transition smoothly into their new property or phase of life.

NOTES

CHAPTER 7

NEGOTIATION STRATEGIES FOR BUYER AND SELLER REPRESENTATION

Buyer Representation:

- Strong Market Knowledge: Leverage your experience to provide accurate market insights.
- Win-Win Approach: Aim for outcomes that satisfy both parties' objectives.
- Positioning Strengths: Showcase your reputation and track record to strengthen your negotiation position.
- Creative Solutions: Suggest creative alternatives to overcome potential deal-breakers.
- Emotional Intelligence: Understand the buyer's emotions and motivations for strategic negotiation.

Seller Representation:

- In-Depth Analysis: Present a comprehensive market analysis to justify your pricing strategy.
- Effective Counteroffers: Craft counteroffers that address concerns while protecting your seller's interests.
- Managing Complexities: Navigate complex situations, such as multiple offers, with finesse.
- Anticipate Buyer Moves: Use your experience to anticipate buyer behavior and respond strategically.
- Collaborative Approach: Collaborate with the buyer's agent to find common ground and reach an agreement.

Objective: To develop an understanding of effective negotiation strategies in both buyer and seller representation scenarios within real estate transactions.

Instructions:

Part I: Buyer Representation

Scenario: Imagine you are representing a buyer who is interested in purchasing a property but is concerned about the asking price.

Task: Develop a negotiation strategy for representing the buyer. Consider factors like the buyer's budget, market conditions, and the property's value. Outline the steps you would take to address the buyer's concerns and achieve a favorable outcome.

Key Points to Include:

- Understanding the buyer's priorities and motivations.
- Gathering data and market comps to justify a counteroffer.
- Presenting a well-reasoned counteroffer that reflects the buyer's interests.
- Using effective communication and persuasive skills to negotiate with the seller's agent.
- Anticipating potential objections and having responses ready

Part 2: Seller Representation

Scenario: Suppose you are representing a seller who has received an offer that is slightly below the asking price.

Task: Develop a negotiation strategy for representing the seller. Consider the property's value, the buyer's offer, and the seller's priorities. Outline the steps you would take to negotiate with the buyer's agent and achieve a successful outcome for your seller.

Key Points to Include:

- Conducting a thorough review of the buyer's offer and their financial capacity.
- Assessing the market conditions and recent comparable sales.
- Crafting a counteroffer that respects the seller's interests while remaining attractive to the buyer.
- Demonstrating the value of the property and addressing potential concerns.
- Employing persuasive negotiation techniques to navigate the counteroffer process effectively.

Lets Try this Exercise

Prepare a written report or presentation that outlines your negotiation strategies for both buyer and seller representation. Include key points, steps, and hypothetical conversations or scenarios to illustrate your approach. Your submission should demonstrate a clear understanding of the negotiation process, effective communication, and strategic thinking in real estate transactions.

GINA NASH

Evaluation Criteria:

- Thoroughness and clarity of negotiation strategies.
- Demonstrated understanding of client priorities and market dynamics.
- Logical progression of steps in the negotiation process.
- Effective use of persuasive communication techniques.
- Application of real estate negotiation principles.

Remember, this assignment aims to enhance your negotiation skills in the context of real estate representation. Approach it as an opportunity to practice your strategic thinking and communication abilities in these scenarios.

Your Approach

CHAPTER 8
ADAPTING TO MARKET CHANGES

Task: Develop a plan for market fluctuations (e.g., increase networking in a slow market).

Exercise: Write down your approach for both a buyer's and seller's market.

____

____

____

____

____

Here are five strategies for real estate agents to excel in a competitive market:

I. Targeted Marketing:

Definition: Tailoring your marketing efforts to reach specific segments of your target audience.

Explanation: Instead of using a one-size-fits-all approach, focus your marketing efforts on the demographics and preferences of your ideal clients. This could involve creating specialized content, using targeted advertising, and engaging with potential clients on platforms they frequent.

2. Exceptional Customer Service:

Definition: Providing outstanding service that goes above and beyond client expectations.

Explanation: Offer personalized attention, prompt responses, and expert guidance to your clients. Building strong relationships based on trust and delivering exceptional value can set you apart in a competitive market.

3. Innovative Technology Adoption:

Definition: Incorporating the latest technology tools and platforms to enhance your services.

Explanation: Stay updated with technological advancements such as virtual tours, 3D property imaging, AI-driven data analysis, and digital marketing techniques. Implementing these tools can impress clients and streamline processes, making you more efficient and effective.

GINA NASH

4. Networking and Partnerships:

Definition: Building relationships with other professionals in the industry and related fields.

Explanation: Collaborate with mortgage brokers, real estate attorneys, home inspectors, and other relevant experts. Strong partnerships can lead to referrals and a more comprehensive service offering, giving you a competitive edge.

5. Market Expertise:

Definition: Deep understanding of local market trends, pricing, and conditions.

Explanation: Becoming an authority on your local market allows you to provide valuable insights to clients. Share your knowledge about neighborhood dynamics, property values, and investment opportunities to showcase your expertise and build trust.

Working in a competitive real estate market requires a strategic approach that emphasizes differentiation, excellent service, and adapting to industry advancements. By implementing these strategies, real estate agents can thrive and stand out in even the most competitive landscapes.

Out of these 5 strategies which do you think you can implement immediately in a changing market and How?

____

____

____

____

Think of another strategy that you think you can use from your own list.

____

____

____

How would you use it?

____

____

____

Best Way to Pivot During Economic Downturns or Industry Shifts as a Real Estate Agent:

Adaptation and Specialization: Identify emerging niches (e.g., distressed properties, investment opportunities) and pivot your services accordingly. Leverage technology for virtual tours, enhance online presence, and provide value through educational content. Emphasize empathy, transparency, and personalized solutions to meet changing client needs.

Exercise: Adapting to Market Changes in Real Estate

Objective: To practice adapting your real estate approach to changing market conditions.

Instructions:

- Choose a Shift: Pick a recent change in the real estate market, like remote work trends or shifting buyer preferences.
- Identify Changes: List how this shift has impacted client needs and market dynamics.
- Spot Opportunities: Note potential niches or services that could emerge due to this change.
- Tailor Services: Brainstorm ways to adjust your services to cater to the new opportunities.
- Use Technology: Explore how technology (like online tours) can enhance your approach.
- Create Simple Content: Write a short post or script explaining the change and how you're adapting to it.
- Practice Communication: Pretend you're explaining the change to a client, highlighting your adapted services.
- Reflect: Consider how this exercise has prepared you to handle real shifts in the future.

Continuing education for a real estate agent refers to the ongoing learning and professional development that agents undertake throughout their careers to stay updated on industry trends, regulations, best practices, and emerging technologies. It's a way to enhance knowledge, skills, and expertise, ensuring that agents provide the best possible service to their clients. Continuing education requirements can vary by region and licensing authority, but the general aim is to keep agents informed and competent in an ever-evolving real estate landscape.

What Name 5 CE Courses you would want to take this year

1. ____

2. ____

3. ____

4. ____

5. ____

CHAPTER 9
SELF-CARE AND WORK-LIFE BALANCE

Managing Stress and Burnout:

- Recognize signs of stress like fatigue and irritability.
- Take breaks and disconnect to recharge.
- Delegate tasks when possible to avoid overwhelm.
- Engage in hobbies or activities you enjoy.

Setting Boundaries and Prioritizing Self-Care:

- Define specific work hours and stick to them.
- Communicate clearly with clients about availability.
- Make time for personal activities and relaxation.
- Treat self-care as a non-negotiable commitment.

GINA NASH

Strategies for Maintaining Work-Life Balance:

- Plan and prioritize tasks for each day.
- Learn to say "no" to avoid overcommitting.
- Allocate time for exercise, family, and friends.
- Use technology to manage work efficiently.

Task: Develop a weekly self-care schedule.

____

____

____

Example: Yoga on Mondays, hiking on Fridays.

- Pros: Reduced burnout,
- Cons: Time management.

Exercise: Write a paragraph on how self-care improves your performance.

____

____

____

These interactive elements, exercises, and tasks will help you actively engage with the material, personalize your learning journey, and apply the concepts directly to your real estate career.

Here's a sample daily schedule for a real estate agent to stay productive and efficient in their business:

Sample Real Estate Agent's Productive Daily Schedule

Morning Routine (8:00 AM - 9:00 AM)	• 8:00 AM: Wake up, exercise, and have a healthy breakfast. • 8:30 AM: Review goals for the day and set priorities.
Prospecting and Lead Generation (9:00 AM - 11:00 AM)	• 9:00 AM: Initiate follow-up calls or emails to leads from yesterday. • 9:30 AM: Cold calling or reaching out to new leads. • 10:00 AM: Research potential leads from different sources (FSBOs, expired listings, referrals) • 11:00 AM: Document and organize lead interactions in CRM.
Property Showings and Client Meetings (11:00 AM - 2:00 PM)	• 11:30 AM: Schedule and conduct property showings. • 12:30 PM: Lunch break and quick check of emails. • 1:00 PM: Meet with prospective or current clients for consultations. • 2:00 PM: Review notes and follow-up actions from meetings
Administrative Tasks (2:00 PM - 3:30 PM)	• 2:00 PM: Respond to emails, answer phone calls, and handle administrative tasks. • 2:30 PM: Update and maintain listings on the MLS and your website. • 3:00 PM: Review and process paperwork for pending transactions.

Marketing and Content Creation (3:30 PM - 5:00 PM)	• 3:30 PM: Develop social media content for the week. • 4:00 PM: Record videos or create virtual property tours. • 4:30 PM: Write blog posts or create market updates for your website. • 5:00 PM: Schedule posts and content for social media.
Professional Development and Planning (5:00 PM - 6:00 PM)	• 5:00 PM: Attend virtual seminars, webinars, or workshops. • 5:30 PM: Review industry news and updates. • 6:00 PM: Set goals and priorities for the next day.
Evening Routine (6:00 PM - 7:00 PM)	• 6:00 PM: Wrap up work tasks and shut down the workspace. • 6:30 PM: Engage in relaxation activities (reading, exercise, hobbies). • 7:00 PM: Enjoy dinner and spend quality time with family or friends.

NOTES

____

____

____

____

Here's a layout of a weekly schedule that a real estate agent can use to stay productive and successful in their real estate career:

Weekly Productive and Successful Real Estate Agent Schedule

Monday: Prospecting and Planning	<ul><li>9:00 AM - 10:00 AM: Review goals for the week and set priorities.</li><li>10:00 AM - 11:30 AM: Prospect and reach out to new leads.</li><li>11:30 AM - 1:00 PM: Follow up with leads from the previous week.</li><li>1:00 PM - 2:00 PM: Lunch and quick email check.</li><li>2:00 PM - 3:00 PM: Attend team or brokerage meeting for updates.</li><li>3:00 PM - 5:00 PM: Plan marketing content for the week.</li></ul>
Tuesday: Client Meetings and Showings	<ul><li>9:00 AM - 11:00 AM: Conduct property showings.</li><li>11:00 AM - 1:00 PM: Meet with prospective or current clients.</li><li>1:00 PM - 2:00 PM: Lunch and respond to urgent emails.</li><li>2:00 PM - 4:00 PM: Negotiate and finalize contracts with clients.</li><li>4:00 PM - 6:00 PM: Research market trends and competitors.</li></ul>
Wednesday: Marketing and Content Creation	<ul><li>9:00 AM - 11:00 AM: Create virtual property tours or videos.</li><li>11:00 AM - 12:30 PM: Develop social media content.</li><li>12:30 PM - 1:30 PM: Lunch and review ongoing marketing campaigns.</li><li>1:30 PM - 3:00 PM: Write blog posts or market updates.</li><li>3:00 PM - 5:00 PM: Schedule and queue social media posts.</li></ul>

Thursday: Administrative Tasks and Networking	<ul><li>9:00 AM - 11:00 AM: Handle administrative tasks and paperwork.</li><li>11:00 AM - 1:00 PM: Connect with industry professionals for networking.</li><li>1:00 PM - 2:00 PM: Lunch and quick email check.</li><li>2:00 PM - 4:00 PM: Update and maintain listings on the MLS.</li><li>4:00 PM - 6:00 PM: Attend virtual seminars or webinars for professional development.</li></ul>
Friday: Client Follow-Up and Reflection	<ul><li>9:00 AM - 10:00 AM: Reach out to clients for follow-up and updates.</li><li>10:00 AM - 11:30 AM: Plan and schedule weekend property showings.</li><li>11:30 AM - 12:30 PM: Review achievements and areas for improvement.</li><li>12:30 PM - 1:30 PM: Lunch and relax.</li><li>1:30 PM - 3:00 PM: Reflect on the week and set goals for the next week.</li></ul>
Saturday: Property Showings and Open Houses	<ul><li>10:00 AM - 4:00 PM: Schedule property showings and open houses.</li><li>4:00 PM - 6:00 PM: Collect feedback from potential buyers.</li><li>Evening: Rest and recharge for the upcoming week.</li></ul>
Sunday: Rest and Planning	<ul><li>Day Off: Spend time with family, engage in hobbies, and relax.</li><li>Evening: Review the past week's activities and plan for the upcoming week</li></ul>

Flexibility is crucial, given that real estate often demands changes to meet client needs and market shifts. Customize this schedule to match your preferences, and allocate time for self-care to prevent burnout. Regularly assess productivity and adjust as necessary for best results. Adaptability matters in real estate, so feel free to tailor the schedule as per your needs, market demands, and preferences. Regularly review goals and accomplishments to stay focused and enhance your success as a real estate agent.

Let's Summarize

Discovering Your Personal Brand as a Real Estate Agent Worksheet

Step I: Self-Reflection and Values

- What values and principles are most important to you in your real estate career?

____

____

- What do you want your clients to associate you with? .

____

____

- List your personal strengths and skills that you bring to the real estate industry.

____

____

GINA NASH

Step 2: **Define Your Target Audience**

- Who is your ideal client? Describe their demographics, preferences, and needs .

  ____

  ____

  ____

- What unique challenges or pain points does your target audience face?

  ____

  ____

Step 3: **Differentiating Factors**

- What sets you apart from other real estate agents in your market?

  ____

  ____

  ____

- How can you provide exceptional value to your clients?

  ____

  ____

Step 4: **Craft Your Brand Statement**

- Combine your values, strengths, target audience, and differentiating factors to create a concise brand statement.

____

____

____

____

____

> **Example: "I am a dedicated real estate agent known for my integrity and data-driven approach. I specialize in helping young families find their dream homes in the suburbs, offering personalized service and expert advice."**

Step 5: **Visual Identity and Communication**

- Choose a color palette that aligns with your brand personality (e.g., professional, approachable).

____

____

____

- Select fonts that reflect your brand's tone (e.g., modern, classic).

____

____

Example: Modern sans-serif for a fresh look, classic serif for timeless appeal

- Create a professional logo that represents your brand's essence

____

____

- List platforms where you'll communicate your brand (website, social media, business cards).

____

____

Step 6: Consistency and Implementation

- How will you ensure consistency in your brand messaging across all platforms?

____

____

- What type of content will you share to reinforce your brand identity?

____

____

Exercise: Defining Your Real Estate Agent Identity and Goals

Objective: In this exercise, you will reflect on your aspirations and intentions as a real estate agent. By the end, you will have a clear understanding of the type of agent you want to become and will have defined your short-term and long-term goals in the real estate industry.

Instructions:

Self-Reflection: Take a few moments to ponder the following questions:

* What motivated you to pursue a career in real estate?

____

____

____

* What qualities or characteristics do you want to embody as a real estate agent?

____

____

____

* How do you envision your role in helping clients achieve their real estate goals?

____

____

____

Define Your Agent Identity: Write a brief statement describing the type of real estate agent you aspire to be. Consider the following aspects:

- Your niche or specialization (e.g., residential, commercial, luxury, property management).

____

____

____

- Your unique selling points or value proposition.

____

____

____

- How you plan to approach client relationships and transactions

____

____

____

> **Example:** "I aspire to be a dedicated residential real estate agent known for my exceptional customer service, in-depth knowledge of local neighborhoods, and commitment to helping first-time homebuyers find their dream homes."

Short-Term Goals: Think about what you hope to achieve in the next 1-2 years in your real estate career. Write down your short-term goals. These could include:

- Achieving a specific number of closed transactions.

____

____

____

- Earning a certain level of commission income

____

____

____

- Obtaining additional real estate certifications or training

____

____

____

- Expanding your network through networking events or social media

____

____

____

Long-Term Goals: Consider your vision for your real estate career in the next 5-IO years. Write down your long-term goals, which might include:

- Becoming a recognized expert in your chosen niche.

____

____

____

- Expanding your team or brokerage

____

____

____

- Diversifying your real estate portfolio with investment properties.

____

____

____

- Achieving financial milestones, such as reaching a specific net worth.

> **Example:** "My long-term goal is to establish myself as the go-to luxury real estate agent in my city, expand my team to three additional agents, and acquire a diverse portfolio of income-generating investment properties."

Share and Discuss: If you're working with a group or mentor, take some time to share your agent identity and goals. Discuss your aspirations and receive feedback and insights from others.

Review and Refine: Periodically revisit and adjust your agent identity and goals as your career progresses. This exercise can be a valuable tool for keeping you focused and motivated on your path to success in real estate.

Remember that your goals may evolve over time, so it's important to adapt and refine them as needed. Your agent identity and goals will serve as a compass, guiding you toward the real estate career you envision for yourself.

CONCLUSION

"In wrapping up this comprehensive journey through the real estate industry, it's evident that success hinges on a harmonious interplay of multifaceted skills, adaptability, and personal well-being. From the foundational knowledge gained in understanding your role and exploring diverse niches to the intricate art of nurturing client relationships and deftly navigating market fluctuations, each chapter has unfurled a critical facet of your professional evolution.

Remember, this voyage isn't solely about acquiring knowledge; it's about wielding that knowledge with precision and strategic finesse. Employing effective marketing techniques, astute negotiation strategies, and a keen eye for emerging market trends will propel you forward. Embracing the concept of adaptability and confidently pivoting during economic downturns or industry shifts will be your compass in uncharted waters.

Yet, amidst the vigorous pursuit of professional growth, never underestimate the power of self-care and maintaining a sustainable work-life balance. By practicing stress management, setting boundaries, and prioritizing personal well-being, you'll ensure that your journey remains not just productive, but fulfilling.

In essence, this is your voyage to shape—a dynamic tapestry woven from your expertise, dedication, and the lessons learned on this educational odyssey. As you step forward into this ever-evolving field, remember that your commitment to self-improvement, coupled with a resilient spirit, will not only secure your place within the real estate industry but also grant you a personally enriching and gratifying career as a real estate agent."

GLOSSARY

40 commonly used real estate vocabulary words along with their simple definitions:

1.Appraisal: An estimate of a property's value conducted by a licensed appraiser.

2. Closing: The final step in a real estate transaction when ownership is transferred to the buyer.

3. Escrow: Funds or documents held by a neutral third party until the closing conditions are met.

4. Title: Legal ownership of a property.

5. Mortgage: A loan to finance the purchase of real estate.

6. Down Payment: The initial payment made by the buyer toward the purchase price.

7. Principal: The amount of the original loan, not including interest.

8. Interest: The cost of borrowing money, paid by the borrower to the lender.

9. Equity: The value of a property minus any outstanding mortgage.

10. Listing: A property that is available for sale or rent.

11. Buyer's Agent: The real estate agent representing the buyer in a transaction.

12. Seller's Agent: The real estate agent representing the seller in a transaction.

13. MLS (Multiple Listing Service): A database of properties listed for sale by real estate agents.

14. Appreciation: Increase in a property's value over time.

15. Depreciation: Decrease in a property's value over time.

16. Home Inspection: A thorough examination of a property's condition.

17. Zoning: Local regulations that determine how a property can be used.

18. Title Insurance: Insurance that protects against loss due to title defects.

19. Contingency: A condition that must be met for a contract to be binding.

20. Offer: A proposal by a buyer to purchase a property.

21. Counteroffer: A response to an offer with different terms.

22.Foreclosure: Legal process when a borrower defaults on a mortgage and the lender takes possession of the property.

23. Deed: Legal document transferring ownership of a property.

24. Real Estate Agent: Licensed professional who assists in buying, selling, or renting properties.

25. Earnest Money: A deposit made by the buyer to show their commitment to purchasing the property.

GINA NASH

26. CMA (Comparative Market Analysis): A report that estimates a property's value based on similar recent sales.
27. Lease: A legal agreement for renting a property.
28. Tenant: The person renting a property.
29. Landlord: The person who owns the property being rented.
30. Condo: A type of property where each unit is owned individually and common areas are shared.
31. Co-op: A housing arrangement where residents own shares in a corporation that owns the building.
32. Apartment: A rental unit within a larger building.
33. FSBO (For Sale By Owner): A property being sold by the owner without a real estate agent. 34. Escrow Account: An account where funds are held for property-related expenses like taxes and insurance.
35. Lien: A claim against a property to satisfy a debt or obligation.
36. Clear Title: A title free from any legal disputes or claims.
37. Capital Gains: The profit from the sale of a property.
38. Pre-Approval: A lender's confirmation of a buyer's ability to qualify for a mortgage.
39. Amortization: The gradual repayment of a mortgage loan through regular payments.
40. Broker: A real estate professional who has obtained a broker's license and can supervise agents.
41. Downsizing: The process of moving to a smaller or less expensive property.
42. Easement: A legal right to use someone else's property for a specific purpose.
43. Multiple Offers: When multiple buyers submit offers on a property simultaneously.
44. Amortization Schedule: A table showing how a mortgage is gradually paid off over time.
45. Title Search: A thorough examination of public records to verify a property's legal ownership.
46. Contingent Offer: An offer to buy a property that is contingent on specific conditions being met.
47. Capitalization Rate (Cap Rate): The rate of return on an investment property based on its income.
48. Homeowners Association (HOA): An organization that manages and enforces rules for a community or development.
49. PITI: Acronym for the components of a monthly mortgage payment: Principal, Interest, Taxes, and Insurance.
50. Conventional Loan: A mortgage loan that is not insured or guaranteed by a government agency.

BOOKS

"The Millionaire Real Estate Agent" by Gary Keller, Dave Jenks, Jay Papasan
- Offers a comprehensive guide to building a successful real estate career and maximizing income.

"Never Split the Difference" by Chris Voss
- Teaches negotiation techniques applicable to real estate transactions.

"The Book on Rental Property Investing" by Brandon Turner
- Provides insights into investing in rental properties and creating passive income.

"Fanatical Prospecting" by Jeb Blount
- Focuses on effective prospecting strategies to grow your client base.

"Crucial Conversations" by Al Switzler, Joseph Grenny, Ron McMillan
- Helps you navigate difficult conversations and negotiations with clients and partners.

PODCASTS

"BiggerPockets Real Estate Podcast"
- Covers a wide range of real estate topics, from investing to agent strategies.

"The Tom Ferry Podcast Experience"
- Hosted by a renowned real estate coach, it provides insights on sales, marketing, and productivity.

"The Real Estate Marketing Dude" Podcast
- Focuses on modern marketing techniques for real estate professionals.

"The Agent Edge Podcast"
- Explores real-world success stories and tips from top-performing agents.

"Real Estate Rockstars" Podcast
- Features interviews with successful real estate professionals sharing their strategies.

ONLINE RESOURCES

National Association of Realtors (NAR)
- Offers a wide range of resources, research, and education for real estate agents.

Inman News
- Provides industry news, trends, and insights on real estate and technology.

Zillow Premier Agent Resource Center
- Offers tips, guides, and best practices for agents using Zillow for lead generation.

REALTOR Magazine
- Offers articles, insights, and practical advice for real estate professionals.

ActiveRain
- A community platform for real estate professionals to share knowledge and experiences.

These recommended books, podcasts, and resources can provide real estate agents with valuable insights, strategies, and knowledge to excel in the ever-evolving industry of 2023.

ABOUT THE AUTHOR

Gina Nash is a distinguished Real Estate Professional and Business Entrepreneur with a diverse background in the mortgage and real estate industries. Born in Shreveport, Louisiana, she began her career in the mortgage sector in 1995, and later transitioned to the real estate sales industry during the mortgage crisis in 2008. Gina's career trajectory showcases her adaptability and expertise in the real estate market.

She holds a Law Degree from John Marshall Law School and a Bachelor of Arts Degree from Grambling State University, which reflects her dedication to higher education and continuous professional development.

As the Owner of Global Realty Partners, a reputable Real Estate Brokerage Firm, Gina specializes in connecting clients with their ideal properties, both private and commercial. Her firm comprises a team of licensed real estate professionals who are committed to delivering high-quality real estate services and providing excellent outcomes to their clients' needs. Her extensive network and experience in the industry have been instrumental in her success as a real estate broker.

Gina has earned a solid reputation among her colleagues and clients for her professionalism, loyalty, integrity, and top-notch customer service, earning her recognition as a top-producing real estate professional by the Atlanta Realtors Association, ranking In the top 10% of professionals in her field.

GINA NASH

With over fifteen years of experience in the Atlanta real estate market, Gina has excelled in achieving sales milestones and is widely trusted and admired as an agent. Her executive staff at Global Realty Partners possess vast knowledge of the Metro Atlanta market, ensuring that clients' needs are met round the clock.

Driven by a passion for the real estate industry and a desire to give back, Gina established Nash Real Estate Academy. The academy aims to mentor and guide new agents, fostering ambition and growth in the real estate sector through continuous education and teaching.

Recently, Gina added a Law Degree to her list of accomplishments, showcasing her dedication to expanding her expertise and services. She plans to integrate her legal services into her already impressive portfolio, further solidifying her position in the industry.

Gina's long-term vision includes continuing to grow her legacy and business, ultimately passing it down to her family. Her unwavering commitment to putting her clients' needs first remains her primary mission, driving her success and esteemed reputation in the real estate market.

www.ingramcontent.com/pod-product-compliance
Lightning Source LLC
Chambersburg PA
CBHW080530130726
47999CB00007BA/2364